Beneficence

Carena del Uno

Rainbows of the Soul...

Flowers of the Heart...

The Rapture of Love...

Beneficence

Carena del Uno
P O Box 1061, Pine, AZ 85544

Table of Contents

1: Becoming

Awake the Dawn

Awake the dawn, O Angels of Consciousness, for morning is come.
Night's winds have exposed the hidden shadows. They are done.
And the White Lotus of Love is rising through Creations Sea
To send forth its Fragrance and Beauty to all humanity.

Be still; be patient; and grateful, O Man, for God's Living Grace
That's seeded in the Purity of Love's angelic lace ---
Will blossom in destined timing by Wisdom's Knowing Sage,
To herald the coming of a Purposeful New Age.

ЕGO to ego

Dear ego:
Thank you for being my sponsor, my sage,
But could you also be my limiting cage –
Entrapping me in my own beliefs
Within my judgments' self-made reefs
That separate me from the greater sea
Wherein other truths are likely to be?

Your brilliance and your shining dazzle my mind
Especially as they appear legitimate and refined.
Am I hypnotized by the "wisdom" you bestow?
Does it really show that you actually "Know"?
Or is it but a reflection of surface shining?
Can you truly dive within Heart's Golden Lining
And greet your Master Ego of yore,
The "I AM" Presence within every door –
Who opens to all that are loving and free
From the illusions separating mind from the Golden Sea

Dear Child: --

Beloved of my Heart -- Don't try to glow
With the little knowledge you think you know,
But look more deeply into Life's evolving play
So that, ultimately, We can be One in the coming New Day.

Follow My Laws

Follow My Laws and I will come back
Live out our Love with goodness and tact
For you mirror your brother and sister too
And this earth is a haven created for you
To demonstrate the kindness and goodness you are
And sprout seedlings that can outshine a star
While spreading their Beauty o'er this fair land
As blossoms of Wonder that honor your hand
And as My Spirit circles through many a world
So will our Peace, Love, and Justice be gently unfurled
Just follow My Laws and Love one another
And this Garden of Creation will bloom like no other.

Weaving Through Mirrors

Look softly at the mirror of emotion that the winds of thought don't make ripples on its waters, for only when the waters of emotion are tranquil, can you see your reflection, and only when those waters are pure, can you see into their depths beyond reflections.

So, when thinking about a situation or a person, make sure that your thoughts are kindly, gentle, and filled with the goodness that the waters between remain tranquil and calm.

Then after you pass through this worldly initiation, will you be able to pass more easily through your psychic world where everything you've created outside of the Law of Good is reversed and returns to you. Only then will You be able to open and be at One with the Wondrous Glories of the Supernal where Truth and Beauty reign in the Purity of God's Conception.

The Golden acCord

To purify oneself, to transmute the Silver Cord into the Golden acCord, one must gradually sublimate the pressured intensities within the will, the mind, and the emotions to harmonize within the field of Divine Love and Trust – then Oneness Be-Comes.

Breathing

What is the important part of breathing --
the in-coming of the breath, the out-coming of the breath,
or the window in between ~ the Be-coming of Oneness with Life??

When the winds of change, the Breath of Nature, reach your garden,
do you dance in their music and is the Dance able to dance Itself??

Become as young as the grass of springtime, soft and flexible.
Smile -- float on the currents of change,
and Live within the Great Partnership of Love's Be-coming.

God Bless --

The Fool of The Tarot

You must first experience the Spirit of Life to become a part of Its Truth and Nobility; then give your love and your will to It, losing yourself in its berth.

But why would you choose and discipline yourself to such a selfless path when you were given the grand Ideas of individuality and superiority? To expand that individuality into a reflection of and a unification with The Supreme Oneness, with the heights, depths, and harmony of the Blessed Seeds of Love, Peace, and unspeakable Knowingness that are forever blooming within You.

Are you ready to become the Fool of the Tarot, walking in trust over the cliff with his little animal self into the Invisible Realms beyond???

Happiness

Happiness, like Love, is born out of heaven's etheric center and cannot be willed or controlled from the outer planes. It breathes from The Within into many forms, like the Joy of a perfect day, the splash of energy that bursts through the soul to fulfill one of its long-awaited dreams, or the contentment of a tiny bird who feels its newborns secure and warm under its wings.   And it can come as slowly as a wave from The Sacred Sea to embrace you, or as quickly as Delight's explosion within you. It has awareness, knowing which expression of itself to take and the proper timing for it to appear. , , Inner, Higher, Consciousness abounds.

"Be still and Know" ~ Become attuned to that vast quietude behind and within creation – that mid-point of all vibration -- and fulfill your Purposeful Destiny in Happiness.

Man the Victorious

Hidden Heroes -- Secret Strivings
Noble Ideals -- Heart-born Tithings

The psychic mountains he climbs that are almost out of reach
And the troughs to which he descends that eventually teach
Bring forth new miracles every day
As love-filled offerings within Life's play....

And with each obstacle that's overcome
Man gains Self confidence to honor The One
Who knows Man's Light-filled Destiny
As a Center of Love in Eternity. . .

Man the Victorious

Simple Metaphysics

To run away from a problem by isolating oneself from it or by blocking the energy of a problem is losing the opportunity of using the destined Di-vine Energy of that problem for growth and evolution. In other words, quoting Manly P. Hall: *"Virtue cannot be attained by hiding oneself from vice. Anything that is an evasion or an avoidance means that we're closing a channel by which the life in us is supposed to come."*

Allow and walk in the Integrity of your Deepest Truth while Trusting in the All-Knowing Wisdom and Beneficence of Life, GOD Consciousness, and Universal Law to guide you toward your Ultimate Purpose.

Fulfilling the Promise

Out from the stars that nurtured me
Into the earth who makes me whole,
I wish to fulfill what I'm destined to be
Through the upliftment of humanity's soul.

We've wandered and waited lifetimes to gain
The pure nobility of Heaven's refrain:
     "One for all and all for One"
As we grow toward the Promise of our ordained Fall
Which will unite our will with God's for the benefit of all
And join His Holy Kingdom wherein we shall become
A newly empowered, wise and beneficent Sun.

From Mankind to Mankind

Look beyond appearances
Seek the Light within
Focus not on differences
All of us are kin.

Dance within Life's rapture
Natural Law upholds
Values determine stature
As peaceful Love unfolds.

So go about the day ahead
With Spirit in your heart
Knowing that the Faith you've wed
Will let God do "His" part

And be at peace, oh lovely child
Life's at your command
Walk in Nature, soft and mild
As mankind evolves into Man.

2: Aspiration and Gratitude

The Temple Etheric

The requisites of the Risen Mount on which the Temple Etheric is built:

> Honor Beingness
> Give Freedom
> Allow Patience
> Building Trust Timing
> Understand Deeply
> Love Infinitely

Love empowers Thought with Grace throughout Be-coming.

When I was a child, I was accepted with love, and through it was given a flowering path to follow – with confidence, wonder and beauty, and a template of goodness to guide me. All this and more is the nurturing moss of my soul's unfoldment – my In-Breathing. Now, in open gratitude, will I build a Temple Etheric wherein the pure Love at Its foundation can waft the sublime Wonders of Light through silent space into the hearts of all that are Be-coming with my out-Breathing of Gratefulness.

P.S. There are no closed doors in this Temple Etheric – only open windows, a roof that envisions the Stars, and an altar in the Heart of Beauty resting on a bedrock of Eternal Purity. Herein I (We) rest in Worshipful Peace when I am my Self.

Humility & Dedication

O man of ego, man of wit,
How do I see you from where I sit?
I thank you and treasure you for your congeniality,
But do you think the Universe is overwhelmed by your personality?

You have performed many wondrous acts
Made possible by your insight and collection of facts,
But what made them most wonderful was the dedication within them
That uplifted your world, your neighbors, and kin.

Never forget where your true energy lies
And the purpose inherent to which it flies;
Then true humility will your works reveal –
The Brilliance of Brotherhood and Love unconcealed.

So continue Your creativity of thought and emotion
That has brought joy and happiness to humanity's ocean
Knowing that all are doing their part, like you,
In honoring Life by manifesting the Good and the True.

My Inside Me

I thank Thee, O Inner Self, for residing in me
For Your delicate words expressing what I see
And Your love of all Nature whose Wonders spread Glory
To reveal Life's Truths within Her flowering story.

I love Your inspirations, Your songs, and Your rhyming,
And how You soften my will to allow Destiny's timing --
And even though I live in this world, often half asleep,
I know Your Loving Wisdom is there to guide me from the Deep.

So, I'm not as afraid to walk through night's shade,
For when it comes to pass, improvements shall be made;
And I'll be able to sing a more grateful and loving song
Within Your arms, O Gentle Soul, where I belong.

This Morning's Prayer

May I be so rooted in love
That the winds of thought
And the waters of emotion
Freely and beneficently give,
Are received in peace
With smiles of gratitude
For their life and the growth
and learning they provide.

A Spring Morning's Words

When the dust of yesterday has loosened its hold
   In the warmth of the morning sun,
And the birds begin to flit from tree to tree,
   The heart swells as the privilege of a new day…

And in it, may I sparkle like the dew on Nature's grassy floor –
May I glide like a soundless breeze among the forest's sweetness –
And may I caress the delicate flowers awakening
   in the beauty of their promise.

Another day of quiet rapture…
  Another day of seeing and being…
   Another day opening Its Goodness to One and All.

God bless you on this Glorious Spring Morn.

Heart's Quiet Song

My heart sings a quiet song
About dreams of trees and visions long
Of birds in flight and wandering deer
And the treasures of nature that are ever near —
Of stars at night and flowering hills
And of evening's peace when all is still.

Oh, earth of wonders, earth of joy,
Thy smile beckons each girl and boy
To go out and play
In the sunshine of each day
Amid the singing waters of the brook
And the seclusion of each wooded nook.

Just remembering those youthful times
Gives one a fullness that quiets yet shines --
The simple beauties of love's tranquil blooming
That breathes in the warmth of Life's finest tuning
And honors all with a quiet dignity
Within the womb of The Mother's Great Sea.

Oh, may we, as gardeners of this world in our keeping,
Live lives of value that it's joys we'll always be reaping,
And that our hearts will ever sing their quiet song
Of loving gratitude to the All of which we belong.

Untethered Within the Beam

Through the night I have made,
I walk without fear, my mind unafraid

For I know that the treasure of the eternal goal
Is the Freedom of Heart joined with the Cosmic Soul.

No grasping after desires in the temporal scene;
No judgments or opinions, just a God centered beam

That shines unconditionally on both evil and good
Timeless in Love, with Life's Quest understood.

Untethered, my patient wings now fly
Into the Brightness of a clear open sky.

The Fullness

O Wondrous Glory, Beauteous Blessings
Living Magnificence, and Tender Caressings
You are The Truth that I seek to become
Bearing a crown that reflects the sun
And a heart that is lovingly One

I thank Thee for Thy Life that allows me to be
A Knowing Part of Your Eternal Sea

Bridging

I want to build a bridge, not a wall,
Between the tall of stature and the small
And stand in its center with arms outstretched
Rejoicing in the dedication of persons doing their best.

I want to watch Life's river carrying Peace and Goodness forward
Within the ordained Destiny of Ideals flowing toward ---
The Freedom of Forgiveness and the Love of Understanding
When Brotherhood has replaced the lust of power's commanding.

I want to see that Bridge of Heart's unification
Evaporate fear's walls of ignorance and separation
That Truth may shine in the Light of Love
Forever uniting our earth with heaven above.

The Privilege of Experience

It's only through life experience that we can rectify our past mistakes, be led to Purposeful Truth, and know the true magnificence of creation. Be grateful for each experience. It is God-given and meant to be lived as a blessing, not feared or struggled against.

The present is a present. Open it and experience its contents with faith and trust as it redeems our Destiny and leads us to our pristine nature. Therein lies our true Reality, the quietude that is at the heart of Zen, that Silence which is the Voice of God before The Word was spoken.

Live a Life of Value

..."not value in terms of consequence,
but Value in terms of Essence..." (Manly P. Hall)

Can you imagine how life could be
if, like the blossoming tree
and the little birds that fly,
Man would dedicate himself to try
to Honor his God and live His Ideals,
opening his world to the Supernally Real --
while seeing the Depth and Beauty in things
and the Wondrous Miracles that Beneficence brings?

No. I don't just want to do something "for" --
I want to become more through my Core.
For while time and polarity has its place,
Heart's singularity unites life with Grace,
And the Values of the True Essence of Life and Living,
Are the Messengers of God's Love that I wish to be giving,

Prayer

May we honor GOD

With every breathe we breathe,
Every thought we think,
And every feeling we feel –

And may our life glorify
the Living Altar of Life.

3: Love

The Ultimate Blessing

LOVE is a state of consciousness.
It needs naught but Itself. It seeks no mirrors.
It is timeless so holds no expectations, yet It withholds nothing.
Linked to The One, It transmutes all unto Itself.
It is GOD's Greatest Blessing.

Awaken, O Voyager

Awaken, O Voyager, from your sleeping
And radiate the sunlight in your keeping.
Let the Love within you so expand
That <u>all</u> of you may understand
Its Golden Heart, so ready to give
It's treasures of Love, that you may live
Your Beneficent Destiny
In the Wondrous Sea of Eternity.

Stars and Flowers

For every caring mind, there shines a star in the sky.
For every loving heart, there blooms a flower on earth.

For every act of kindness,
A young bird sings a new song

And for every prayer of gratitude,
The world breathes in the peace for which it longs.

Gifts of the Peaceful Heart

The Faith of a child as it takes the hand of its parent
The Peace of the deep as it recognizes the fullness of its Being
The Breath of a spring breeze as it awakens Earth to Her potential
The Trust of a flower as she opens her delicate petals to release the
Beauty of her heart
And the Love of Perfect Timing that parts the Veils of Blessings
patiently awaited

These are the simple Wonders that caress our lives each day,
quietly honoring The Giver of Goodness in their Dedication to Love.

From Fear to Love

I was scared, so I only saw what I was afraid of: selfishness & mistakes,
judgment & blame – and I knew they would cause pain…
But I did nothing – until – I saw children crying for help in their
ignorance, and grieving hearts praying to God ----- GOD…

Then I remembered God and Love, and the warm breath of Love
breathed on me: Compassionate Love – Higher, Wider, Deeper, and
Freeing yet more Inclusive than any judgement or law…

And Love embraced my world, and I saw sunlit hearts and helpful
hands, and compassionate blessings. . . And there was no more fear, only
little kids learning to love.   And I loved them all, wanting only the best
for them. And I gave them my heart --- and Healing Peace and
Goodness were <u>ours</u> all-ways and for-ever.

ps. Who would believe that "negatives" are but touchstones to Love…

Heart's Song

As gently as the snowflake glides down to her rest,
As softly as the newborn flowers her nest,
That is the Song Heart sings to you
In the Goodness of Life that remains ever True.

Love's Purgatory

Upon awakening into the borderline state, I thought of my life's regrets, and this is what came:

We wear clothes to close off and protect our physical bodies
from exposure to worldly judgement. Isn't it possible, then,
 that we also wear psychic clothes (close) to protect our mental
and emotional bodies from being exposed to that judgement?

At some time in our lives, however, we must look at these undesirable
clothes, take them out of our emotional waters, wash them, and let them
dry by hanging them out on a line so that the emotions that befell them
can evaporate in the sun.

There is Love in the freeing of secret blames, and Freedom in the
understanding Knowingness of Forgiveness. . .

The God within has blessed us all with Love.
					Now it's up to us to learn Forgiveness.

Love's Resonance

A person cannot feel love from another source if that person didn't already have love within them. What makes a loving feeling so special is the resonance of two or more loves combined, for that resonance automatically intensifies the loving energy frequencies manyfold.

It matters not with resonance whether you are the giver or the receiver, nor does it matter if the giver and the receiver are both on the physical plane or if one is on a different plane. As you give love through your soul heart, it will be received by a one or a many who need it, thus the conditions for the building up of that love energy through resonance exists. That is one reason why when you selflessly offer up a prayer of thanksgiving, you can feel an exultation as it is echoing through the inner spaces.

So, this holiday season, remember to send out feeling prayers of gratefulness that the love within you be resonated by those in need who are receiving it and who will join you in its natural, glorious upliftment... Joy to the world!

Reverence

It's easy to find reverence in a forest cathedral or beauty in a palace of gold, but think, oh wondrous man, on the cut flower that still opens its heart in reverence to add to the beauty and love of creation.

True living lies within the miracle of Love. Sing the silent song of reverence to the heart of all you see, and catch the breath of Glory that opens and fulfills all life.

The Marriage

You can call me incestuous or gay,
But I did nothing I regret that day. . .
While in a morning hike atop a tree feathered hill,
I rested amidst wild flowers, golden and still --
Scattered by Mother Nature in her ever-giving way
To bless earth, the beautiful, with her Love in play.

So sacred was the feeling of Her Being, so true and whole,
That I prayed that all people feel this Presence within their soul.

While sharing a few drops of water with the flowers close to me,
I hoped that the others could drink from The Mother's Great Sea –
Then while ambling down the path, after saying Good-bye,
A wave of such Love infilled me, making my eyes actually cry,
From the Goodness, the Blessings, and Loving care
That were almost too Wondrous for me to bare…

It was then that it happened, our Vows were sacredly tied,
In a Marriage between Mother Nature and I, the humble bride!

Then, to seal the Bond of Joy reigning down from above
I ate a tiny daisy as my communion of Love,
And glided reverently down the mountain,
Cherishing a memory never to be forgotten.

PS:
Later that afternoon, though such weather was not anticipated,
a small rain caressed our hills -- Mother Nature had participated
in watering her siblings, her bright golden flowers,
and swelling my heart as part of her dower.

Interdependence

Interdependence – hands united in friendship and caring around the world; trees communing through their Mother by their cores and roots; and animals speaking in silence through their subtle inner sensing. Even air, the great intermediary, though weightless and transparent, is yet full of the essences needed to sustain life, synergistically weaving itself between and within all that is – even allowing light to dance in its winds and water to cascade through it down great cliffs as it regales rainbows in the sunlight. So is there great interdependence within the seen and unseen.

GOD has willed this land to flower and perpetuate itself in beneficence and harmonious interdependence. One day, when the concept of fear has evaporated in the sunlight of love, will the interdependence of all creates spiral back into the Oneness that is its birthright, and each will carry with them the Fullness of themselves and the Allness of that which lives eternally.

May we rejoice in our Inheritance and be grateful for our Heart's Interdependence with All That IS.

Streams of Love

Streams from Heart's foreverness
Through our eyes come blessing,
Ever waiting to honor their loves
With their soul's caressing.

O The Wonder of that communion
That breathes through our heavenly realm
As it shares the Beauty that resides
With Truth and Purity at Its helm

We thank thee, O mortals,
For thy openness to receive
The Love and the Goodness
That Omniety conceived

As we honor you this waking day
And every day to come
With streams of Love Joyously sent
From Heart's Eternal Sun.

The God Within You

What's your conception of God, the Great One Denominator?
Be it a Consciousness of fulfilling Love, peaceful Beneficence,
Freedom, Wisdom and Justice?
If God is truly the Great One Denominator, all that & more is within
you.
Be His Cup, His Altar, His Sanctuary, and His Love expressing.

Bless Him as He Blesses you.

Comfort in God

I want God's Consciousness to be comfortable
     when I'm close to Him ---
I don't want Him to feel my nervousness
Or be saddened by my imperviousness
But to be gladdened at my presence
While radiating His Love-filled essence.

Then after moments of peaceful union,
I'll glide to earth to resume my communion
With the Spirit he has sent
To all who are heaven bent –
Grateful for the Magic infilling the below and above
That's ever flowing from His Center of Love.

The Peace of Expansion

Dear Friends,

I was feeling isolated this morning as I was waking up, and found the focus of my mind in a central point in my head – Then that point expanded into the memory of all the wonderful things and people who were and are still, even now, in my life, and then it further expanded beyond where there was no limitation, just a wondrous sense of wholeness, and the isolated point was no more -- And the Breath of Life seemed to breathe Itself inside of me. This is what came:

The Peace of Expansion

Every thought of Love,
Every feeling of Love,
Every creation of Love
In Being, in Memory, in Consciousness
Is here now when you
Open yourself,
Free yourself,
Evaporate yourself
Into the Expanse that Is, was, and ever will be.

I Didn't Understand

I didn't understand when my parents quarreled.
I took sides.

I didn't understand when starving people did almost anything for money.
I took sides.

I didn't understand when a man who was scared and hurting inside tried to hurt others.
I took sides.

Love understands and doesn't take sides. It quietly tries to bring everything – every thought, every feeling, every being – into Itself. Allow Love to hold you in Its arms, bring you to Its depth of understanding, and discover the great potential of Its beneficence.

Your Birthday

41

Every day's a Birthday
When in the Light of Love,
Quickened by the angels

And the stars above.

Yes, the body's getting older,
But that is not the thing,
That honors You and the God within
About which the Universe sings.

Your song of love came down with you
When you took your very first breath
And glorified humanity's throng
That heaven and earth be blessed.

So carry on your mission,
Dear and beautiful friend,
For by your giving of Your Heart's Love
It's Joy and Goodness will never end.

To a Loving Christmas

Love flows invisibly along etheric golden ribbons
Uniting everybody into everyOne ~
And arms open wide,
And hearts expand,
And joy caresses the air…

It's Christmas
And the Hands of the Christ
Are blessing each of His children
With their heart's delights
As the Spirit of Giving births itself
Once again throughout the land.

May God bless you with a Merry Christmas.

Polarity's Potential

The deeper the darkness I walk through

The greater the Light that will ensue

Within the womb of Love.

4: Mother, Nature, Earth

Our Mother

Within Her planet of Wonder
The Mother spreads her living grace
As the sky abounds with music and stars
And the earth with Beauty is laced.

Birds sing as they wing through the bushes and trees
And meadows of flowers flow like waves rolling at sea --
Life blooms around us, reaching to the sun,
Joyous in its reverence to Glorify The One.

No matter the cost, God's Integrity is there,
To proclaim Life in Goodness, Its Lovingness to share
A Template of grandeur, open and free
Awaiting the coming of the Perfection of Me –
A gardener of Lovingness, with the caretaker's duty
To honor and enhance creation's miracles of
Truth.
Purpose, & Beauty.

GOD Bless

Every leaf of grass that grows
Every tree that breathes
Every bird that flies
And every creation within The Mother of Being
With the Beneficence
Bestowed by the Love of The Father.

Breathing in Divinity

Mother Nature and Her Love lives in the heart of me
Not just in the gardens my eyes can see
So from deep in my being do I reverently vow
To honor Her Gentle Lovingness that I feel now
And protect Her from any thought that might come to me
That would give Her pain or pollute Her nurturing sea.

--- --- ---

Like the Holy Spirit centered between God and Man
Does Christ's Lovingness take Its stand
To unite the aspiring soul of humanity
Within the embrace of His Divinity
While also honoring His Father's Purity
And the Loving Beneficence that shall ever be
Throughout time and eternity.

Forest Communion

I go into the forest with my mind
And come out with my heart. . .

Saying a silent prayer of thankfulness, I become part of the welcoming trees as I gently walk to my meditation rock, there to find Peace in the depths of us.

I am like the tiny wild flower nestled in the grass beside the infinite path of Life – opening my arms, my petals, to the heavens as I gaze upward and give myself to the Mother's Great Cosmic Garden of Love. I know I am small, but She feels me and fills my heart beyond boundaries as we become One in silent communion. Time disappears.

Then, slowly, when time and breath become real once again, I open my eyes to the brightness of the forested earth that surrounds me, and, lifting myself from my rock, I stretch out my arms in gratitude to the All That Is and let my heart carry me home.

O Glorious Nature

O Glorious Nature ~
I stand at your gateway in awe,
my arms outstretched in openness,
to feel the peaceful reverence of your kindly trees.

And, as each hand touches their protecting bark,
my heart expands into the Fullness of You,
my mind breathes the silent rapture of Oneness,
and I am whole.

You are truly the Handmaiden of GOD
Inspiring all to arise through earth's nourishing sod
To become the reflection of the Template they are meant to be
Within Creation's Wondrous Sea.

And in my hours of quiet and humble rest
When I commune with Thee, I feel truly blest
As together, we can share GOD's beauteous treasure
Of Life, Light, and Love beyond measure.

Leaves from the Soul

I sit in the middle of a circle of trees each day throughout spring and summer to honor them and their Wholeness in God, for they have acknowledged my Center, my Wholeness, and the True Love that lives in the Heart of each of us.

And now, in autumn, as winter approaches, Mother Nature calls her children unto Her bosom -- and the trees give forth their leaves to Her in glorious colorful arrays in celebration as their life force descends to the roots of their being,
and the animals prepare their nests to meet the stillness of the land, and a natural white peace and purity begins to cover the land. Even the energies of the sun are quieted as they descend into a state of tranquility and rest in the arms of The Mother.

And as each tree relinquishes its leaves to float to the ground, nourishing Mother Earth so that She may resurrect them in a new cycle of becoming, they do so with beauty and grace, and with a trust akin to unending love at their gentle descent -- for fear of change is unknown to them as they are fulfilling the innate Law of their Being... And though the essence of some trees may leave behind their shells during this coming wintry cycle, the fullness of their Beauty will live on in the Eternal Now.

Oh, to have the consciousness of a Tree -- accepting, allowing, giving of itself and its peace, in Oneness with all of its forest kin while honoring The Mother and aspiring to The Father.

Dear grace-filled and noble trees, we thank thee for thy presence, thy essence, and for allowing us to commune with thee in a depth of Being that knows naught but the Fullness of Love.

My Forest Cathedral

How can one convey Love, Reverence, and Oneness in words that must be translated by mind on their journey to heart? Could this haloed trinity be felt by those meeting their lifelong companion for the first time, or by those truly devoted to the fullness of their faith when taking communion? Love – Reverence – Oneness. For me, it is softly walking, alone, into my forest cathedral and becoming one therein.

How did I come to this beautiful place of quietude, rapture, and oneness? I don't really know. What I do know is that I gave myself to it, wholly and completely – without seeing trees, bushes and rocks and sky in their separateness, but in their wholeness -- united – Mother Nature dressed in her finest gown – and thus we shared a wHoly Communion.

The hour was approaching 5 in a springtime evening. The sun had begun to nestle itself in the mountains to the west and was gently back-lighting the trees and tall grasses that lay before me. The green grasses and sparkling pine needles were delicately glowing as I walked up the narrow and almost forgotten path. They were so beautiful that I had to pause several times to admire them. At the end of that path, before stepping into beautiful young sprouting trees and the forest beyond, stood two tall, magnificent pine trees, one on each side of the trail. They were like living gate keepers, steadfast and protecting of the forest cathedral beyond.

I couldn't help but stand, almost transfixed to admire that which was before me – and, laying one hand on each tree trunk, I gave thanks. Moments later, an overwhelming gratitude engulfed me. I closed my eyes to envision an encompassing light within my consciousness that was made full by my heart – not a light as we know it, that you can see with your eyes, but a fuller <u>colorless</u> golden light. Was it a sharing of the heart of the two trees, the forest beyond, or of the essence of all forests with my heart? All I know is that I will always honor Mother Nature and her forest cathedrals with every element of my being.

Shortly after returning home, in the fullness of my forest memory, the following poem floated through my mind. I entitled it Communion.

> Lost within the forest's worshipping throng,
> I gave my Self the freedom for which it longed,
> And with arms outstretched between two noble trees
> In Love's communion, together we breathed –
> A rapture of Oneness beyond heart, mind, and soul
> A sunburst of the Power through which Destiny unfolds.
> And in that Givingness behind all giving
> We shared the Glory that lives in all living.

So that you would know truly that all creation, all creatures, flora and fauna, are connected within Love and Being, I will now share with you something personal. One month prior to my communion in the forest cathedral, I fell over a log and broke one or more ribs on my right side. Not a day or night went by that I wasn't aware of their pain – but after my deep communion in my Forest Cathedral, the pain was gone! I thought it was a temporary high, but to this day, my ribs carry no pain -- no pain when I'm rolling over on them in bed; no pain when I take a deep breath; and no pain when I rub or press on the area of the former break.

Dear Friends, we are living in the presence of Miracles every day, be they within a secluded forest, in a quiet church, or in the arms of a child. Miracles? Or simply the wonders of natural laws at work when we can go into the places of our hearts that contain them and be one with them in Love and Reverence. Try, therefore, to put your minds at ease. Sublimate your pressures and quiet your thoughts by closing your eyes and gently intoning the sound "Aum" or "Om", silently or aloud. Feel your Integrity with Being. Open your arms outward on each side of your body with your hands open yet relaxed; then feel your heart open as you appreciate the blessedness that surrounds you.

May you step through the Portal to your Cathedral.

Carena del Uno

Earth

O how could my mind put you, dear Earth
Below Air, Fire, and Water's intrinsic worth?
For within You, true Oneness eternally reigns
Yet supports the finite beings in which we came.

EARTH

It's a privilege and an honor to be here, O Wondrous Earth
To be welcomed with Grace at our Moment of Birth.
You've so much Beauty and Love within your Core
And a Heart that beats true, while opening a Door
To the invisible realms beyond mind's perceptions
Through Daath's White Rose of Purity and It's conceptions.

O may we lose the density of our mundane sight
And open unto Earth's bright inward Light
Where the Spirit of Love nurtures far beyond our knowing
And expands into infinite dimensions of Cosmic sowing.

Dear and Noble Earth, I am honored to have been allowed to
see true
And throughout my days, will cherish the Ephemeral Wonder that is
You.

Mother Earth and me

Seeds of Love, seeds of Goodness —
tender caring and selfless sharing
emanate from our Mother Earth
whose consciousness sublime
for eons of time
has been awaiting Man's rebirth.

Linked together in Purpose by soul and heart,
Take Earth for granted but contribute your part
To honor Her Consciousness in a gentle loving way
That Her Gracious Beauty will always display.

Let go of the selfishness that short-sighted thought is polluting
And turn to the Immaculate Values that Eternity is rooting,
Giving Love back to your Mother and fulfilling <u>Her</u> needs
By your kindness to all in Thought, Word, and Deeds.

The Mother's Gift

The Mother spreads her flowers far and wide
For in delicate Beauty, She would abide
In trees woven from patterns on high
And meadows of grass to wave at the sky.

How wondrous is our life down here
Within Her caresses ever so near
As we breathe Her Breath in the morning breeze
And smile at Her clouds floating with ease.

A God-given Garden, Our Mother has birthed
By immersing Her Self within the body of earth.

So the next time you walk between sky and trees
Feel your Mother and Her Love's patient ease
Her open Heart and gentle hand
And Her limitless offering to all nature and man.

Life is a Sanctuary

Life is a Sanctuary of privileges and powers fulfilled by the moral and ethical values that creation inherited from the Divine Will. And this Sanctuary, while It can rise to the pinnacle of the highest ideal, can also become an invisible, weightless blanket of quietude and peace, as The Spirit of Being nurtures each and embraces both – Breathing Its Beneficence unto the Soul of Life.

Stand in awe, O Man, that you were given the privilege of Life. Worship in Its Sanctuary with dedicated Goodness that you may feel and Know Its Innate Love.

5: Openness, Allowing, Acceptance

Living Life

Allow the day to live itself,
Putting force and impatience on the shelf,
For as you share the natural rhythm if the day,
You're letting vibratory resonance guide your way,

Making this a habit whenever you can
Will give you the Peace of the Inner Man,
And allow the Heart to wed the Mind,
So that harmonic Destiny can replace mechanical time.

Life Lives Itself

When one strives only to fulfill outer wants, ambitions, and desires, he is not truly living Life, but existing outside of his Self and the Fullness of Life.

Life lives Itself. Its livingness feels like floating in the breeze of God's energy field, allowing its breath to take you to your ordained destinations while giving you your lessons in Becoming and the Knowingness of the Magic of Divine Order.

Be at Peace. The Grace of God embraces you with Beneficent Justice, Love, and Wisdom. You will only draw unto yourself what you need to become who You really are. Fear not. Dance.

Mirror, Mirror

Mirror, Mirror on the Wall,
Do you contain a Magic that tries to enthrall
Is it you who has woven our created world
Into mundane desires willfully unfurled?
Did you give man the self-made right
To manifest illusions within his night?

Or is there a Divine Tapestry that Love doth weave
With The Purpose and Values that Higher conceived –
A Tapestry of Holiness through that shines God's Light,
Which, as part of Him, is Man's birthright –

Did this dichotomy come to be
By the Beneficent Intention that each being be free
To choose his self's path through his earthly mind
Or seek his Oneness within Truth Divine?

Please know, fellow traveler, you can't live both,
For before you came, you took an oath
To honor your Creator and the Truth that shall be
In the Wondrous Firmament of This Created Sea.

So where that might give you pause and trepidation,
It also guarantees your eventual salvation.
Therefore, balance yourself on this threshold of life
And allow God to Will HIS Destiny free from strife

For the Harmony within His Beneficent Plan
Can never be defeated by the hand of man
And Immaculate Love and Perfect Timing
Will blossom forth in Eternity's lining
As you gentle yourself in Patience and Trust
And allow God's Guidance to do what It must.

The Obsession of Possession

O possession, what hast thou done to me,
Thinking that even God's Love, so wondrous and free,
That guides me to where It can best serve Its own
Is mine because it came into my physical home.

But, GOD, I am learning at last to let go
And float on Your Breath in earth's manifest show,
Knowing that You lead me to where there's a need
And that it's Your Energy that christens each deed.

So let me be allowing of the energy changes,
Of the comings and goings that Your Love wisely arranges
Within the ordained patterns of Time's tapestry of living
That express Love's true freedom, grace, and selfless giving.

Dear Friends:
Enjoy Spirit's Fullness that may come for but moments in time
Knowing that It's eternal and ever awaiting you in The Sublime.
God bless —

Allow the Open Door

Only when you give up pushing for your desires can they truly fulfill themselves. Only when you cease struggling to remember something, will it come to you. Using mental or emotional pressure keeps your wishes in the realm of human consciousness. For perfect manifestation, you must completely release your wants and desires to the higher plane of creative consciousness and then, with patience, trust & openness, accept the out-come. Thus, does every-thing, every e-vent (energy vent) come as a gift in harmony and perfection through your union with That Which IS.

Release to Peace

I float in a pool of deep quietude
Where n'er a thought can willfully intrude
There to find the peace of release.

Here lies the sanctuary of the natural world
Which, like a breeze, is gently unfurled,
Revealing its sweet core of Being
Through Heart's inward seeing.

It's like removing a veil of dust from your eyes
Whereby the Energy of Life is no longer disguised
But passes through the cells of grass, trees, and leaves
Like tiny rays of sunlight in all you perceive –

'Tis a Wonderland of Beauty, everywhere,
Almost more than your mind can bear,
Freeing your arms to open and outwardly spread
As your heart and that of Nature are lovingly wed. . .

And the Sun kisses your brow,
Briefly, but in the Eternal Now.

Enlightenment

Something is good or bad according to our mind's limited perception of it, and its intensity is determined by the intensity of the emotions we have placed on it. To be still is to let go of the pushing of our attitudes toward it or the blocks we have made (or are making) resisting it.

"Sorry GOD – You aren't manifesting this portion of life the way I want You to. I'm taking over…"

. . .Be still and know that I am GOD.

Walk the middle path, allowing the ups and downs while focusing (with the Clarity of Light) on the Greater Picture of Purposeful Fulfillment.

Peace Be Unto Thee. . .

Timing

I worship the perfection of God's synchronized timing
Encouraging me do what's needed while the sun is shining -
Putting nothing off that should be done today
To satisfy my desires to eat, rest, or play.
And as I honor this Divine aspect in me,
A far more efficient world will I come to see.

Nothing ever happens by chance
For we're living in the music of God's Purposeful Dance.
So, waltz with me through time and space
And enjoy the wonders we're destined to embrace.

Accept Life

Accept Life
I have plans for you…
Know its Wonder
And Greatness too.

Time is a transient thing.
Let Harmony sing
Throughout your eternity
With Beauteous Simplicity.

Love.

Let It Come To You

Be it beautiful or a lesson you've earned,
Let it come to you.

Release the tension coating your seeking eyes;
Become open, peaceful, and heart wise –
Let Life come to you.

And like the Breath that flows out from your soul
Will you know you're becoming Whole. . .

Let God come to you.

Allow Experience

Friends are free-ends
With wills of their own
Who've earned the right
To experience what they've sown

And, as experience is our greatest teacher,
Allow each man to be
The student and director
Of their own reality.

Allow Life

Push not, fight not, fear not,
Or you'll create in yourself a near-sighted knot.
Instead,
      Wed
           Life's Destiny.

For Its Purposeful Organization
Is geared to growth and emancipation ---
That you may recognize each Day of Living
As a bountiful Blessing of Giving
And know the Wonders inherent in The Sanctuary of Creation
Birthed from God's Wholeness and Loving Ideation.

6: Perspectives

The Great Perspective

There are countless finite perspectives and electives --

Chances; dances, and interwoven circumstances,

But True Life and Creation were born of One Law and Principle

And only by living It's Great Perspective can one be invincible.

So instead of focusing on fractions of The Whole,

Consider Life's Purpose and resonate with Its Goal

That the numerous particulars in your destined world

might be harmoniously united and Truth be unfurled.

The Grand Ascension

Mind speaks:

Like the Light of a star
Shining from afar
The Higher Plane calls to me
Distant though it may be
I will refine and set myself free.

I will ascend!

Heart Speaks

With the loving acceptance of a mother for her own
I open myself to all in God's earthly home
Then One with Love Supreme
We become an infallible team
Fulfilling an Eternal Dream

As we ascend together.

The Heart Sings

The Buddhist Doctrine says The Heart Sings

What would be so important to me
That I would stop my Heart's singing?

What would be so important to me
That I would stop the petals of a flower from opening?

Honor the opening ~
Sing Heart's Song ~
Breathe the Fragrance
Of Love Everlasting.

May my soul ever sing within me…

Feel

Feel the loving smile of the sun's first rays as it awakens a new day.
Feel the petals of the tiny flower opening to receive its warm caresses.
Then sing a song of Love to the woodland trees
and feel their echoing appreciation.

Myriad wonders live in the simple heart of Being.
Gentle thyself in I
Its tender Peace.

Feel the Fields

Your physical positions can influence your perspectives' conditions:

To align your mind to the Ideals of Higher
To which the world doth nobly aspire
> *Put your hands fully together in front of your heart,*
> *fingers pointing upward in the attitude of prayer,*
> *close your eyes and allow the energy stream*
> *to lift your consciousness*

To open your heart to its beauteous peace
and Mother Earth's fullness never to cease
> *Touch your fingertips together in the prayer position,*
> *while keeping a round openness between your palms,*
> *with eyes closed and floating in the divine field.*

Then, after these energy fields have been felt and known,
marry them in the wondrous space into which you have grown
> *By gently opening wide your arms to humbly receive*
> *the influx of God's Life in Love's Harmony conceived.*

Dis-Crimination

If we didn't have it in us,
We couldn't recognize it.
If we couldn't re-cognize it,
We couldn't understand it.
If we couldn't under-stand it,
We couldn't not judge it.

Non-judgement is in a neutral space
Wherein Peace is centered in angelic lace
And the Marriage of Mind and Heart takes place.

So relax your imagined fears, knowing challenges are steps in learning
For through them, compassionate understanding you will be earning
And in its freedom, you can attune to your soul's living light
Where Love and Allowing will make your world bright.

Honor the Fabric of Life.
It was spun with infinite care and perfection.

Fear Exposed

The human mind thinks of loss and gain
while the Heart divine sings love's refrain.

For it knows fear will pass by
as an illusion of thought's eye

that sees not beyond the surface of things
and the beneficent creations that God's Truth brings.

So, forgive the ignorance of the some
who know not the Wonders of The One

And go about your daily life
free from doubt, fear and strife.

Morning Musings

Mine and Thine

When you get tired of going in the "mine" field,
Go into the Haven of the Heart
Where you need only to yield
To the Purposeful Good that God doth impart.

Black and White

The black candle's light is just as bright
As that of the white
While both are giving of themselves
On the Altar of God

The Fall

The Fall was a Gift, a Divine Birthright,
That was bestowed upon man to augment his Light.
'Twas neither sinful nor dark
But a Gift of God to kindle a spark
Of greater knowingness, understanding, and wisdom
For the birthing of young gods to rule their kingdom.
A Gift that would lead them to their Core's True Center
That would preside over each willful space that they might enter.
And though this Center be immaculate and indescribable,
It exists eternally, is ever present, and wholly reliable.
Lighter than air, more compelling than life, purer than thought or feeling,
In this Oneness of God, only Love and Beneficence is congealing.

Provide Patience

What's the gift of half hour of patience in eternity?
A breath of kindness ~
A caring ~
A love-filled peace . . .

Accept – Allow – Flow --

Let your moments become invisibly momentous
as you allow the outer rays of time to return to their eternal source,
and you, yourself, gain the gift of freedom that comes from
the knowing of the purposeful oneness in all that Is.

7: Knowing Me

All I See is in Me

All I see is in me:
The heights of heaven above
And the beneficent beauty of love –
The hallowed depth of valleys' deep
And the sacred waters of the oceans' keep –
But, most of all, the Light that shines within our hidden Knowing
That propels us onward to purposeful sowing.

So lend an ear if what you hear is fear
And look at it carefully with a mind that's clear
That you may go through its gate and evaporate
The hidden mistakes that caused you to forsake
The Love and Wisdom that was always by your side
To eventually become the Integrity in which now abide.

Like a Tree

I don't push; I don't pull.
I don't insist, nor do I resist.
I don't compete nor retreat –

Like the noble redwood and healing pine,
Time and eternity are mine. . .
So I stand in my essence
In tune with Omnificence

And Peace issues freely through my being
For I fight not with anything seeming.
Thus, has the spirit of war closed its door
And died on my world's floor..

May the blue of the sky embrace you
And the breath of the Mother fill your heart
As you stretch your arms apart
With the Joy and Wonder of Life.

Our Energy

Is our personal energy truly our own
Or has it been borrowed and is only on loan –

Changing and evolving through time and space
Within the challenges we've caused to embrace?

Knowing that Resonance guides our living choices
We pray for the day we exchange our clamoring voices

For the Peace, Love, and Beauty of The Undying Word.

What is Me and Mine?

Are these words of wisdom and rhyme
Chosen by music and time really mine
Or are they but flowers fashioned in a bouquet
Bestowed by Heaven to enhance creation's display?

In truth, I wonder if my "me" is really mine
Or just part of the flow of Love's spiritual wine
To uplift our total Beingness to the Living Grace
That reflects the Beauty of The Great Mother's Face

Dear GOD,
    Take this little bird within the heart of me
    And fly it to its destiny
    Where it will live in the fullness of Knowing
    Of its Oneness with You and Your Beneficent sowing.

You are Exquisite

The fragrance of Beauty in a flower unborn
The silence of Quietude in hearts to adorn.

Music sings in rocks, hills and plains
Honoring the Majesty from which they came

All this is within your nurturing Spirit
So be thee at peace – You are Exquisite.

Dear Diary

As we are all one, I know not which mind or which consciousness, shared this experience with me. It might have been yours.

As I was awakening, my eyes, still closed to the breaking light of day, found themselves in an unpleasant state of darkness. Then I thought of the beauty of Nature and, specifically, of a rose, and instantly I found myself within its tubular stem. But still feeling uneasy, I tried to bring in harmony, acceptance, and balance to lighten the energy. Nothing worked. Then I opened myself to Honor, honoring God, His Creation, and that which IS, whereupon I realized that I was subliminally seeing an illusion – an illusion that was paper thin and diaphanous, and, even though through my prior anxiety, it made a little thorn on the outside of my path/my tube, the illusion dissolved with my realization of its intangible reality. Then, without trying, I kept going, up in mind and inward in heart, aiding a consuming purpose of which I was unaware. This process continued until, at last, I felt myself enter the realm of Beauty, and, as that Beauty washed over me, I was at peace. I know not how long I floated in this gentle, wonderful, loving peace, but finally I opened a more awakened part of my subliminal consciousness to find myself to be a soft and lovely, beautifully opened rose.

Enjoy your Peace, your Beauty, and your Love this day in Eternity, knowing that the Beautiful, though invisible, White Rose, known by many as Daath, is within you, me, and all of us..

God Bless.

I am in all

I am the little girl with a broken doll
I am the landlord who had a fall
I am the flying man on the high trapeze
And I am the child sleeping with ease.

I am the screams of pain becoming cries of delight
When out of my closet, I walk toward the light
I am the night; I am the day
As each is necessary for the roles I play:

The broken doll, the high trapeze
The wise man, the fool, living as they please
The mother tenderly nursing her young
The father working out under the sun –

For I am all in all, cycling into The One
All life and all seasons since time begun.
But how, pray tell, can this be true?
Through the Miracle of Love united in You!

You Are a Miracle

You are a miracle that's evolved to a stage
Where your mind and emo6tions can be free of self's cage
And seed Truth's Wonders that will help man to climb
Unto his full potential, his inheritance divine.

The All Potential

O Wondrous Being that you are, infilled with all potential ---
Tell me
  Of the mighty oak and the protection that it gives,
  Of the noble redwood and the purposeful aspiration that it
  shares,
  Of the tiny wildflower in its vulnerability, trusting in the love
  that it breathes,
  And of the new mother nurturing her baby through her heart of
  love.

These attributes are all yours, O Man, and more,
                    Otherwise, you couldn't re-cognize them.

'So be at Peace, for you have the potential of be the Glory of God:
    Protected, purposeful, trusted, and loved as a One in The One.

8: Oneness

In the Womb of Oneness

In the Womb of Oneness
Before the birthing tide
Before the living polarity
In which creations abide

Lives a joyous Rapture
Behind the ken of Mind
The Immaculate Generation of Life
From Spirit's Source Divine.

O may Its Holy Conception
In Man be lovingly instilled
That lives be lived within God's Plan
And Destiny be fulfilled.

Communion

Lost within the forest's worshipping throng,
I gave my Self the freedom for which it longed,

And with arms outstretched between two noble trees
In Love's communion, together we breathed –

A rapture of Oneness beyond heart, mind, and soul
A sunburst of the Power through which Destiny unfolds.

And in that Givingness behind all giving
We shared the Glory that lives in Living.

Fulfillment

There will come a time when singing, the words will sing themselves,
The heart will resound with the Pulse and Beauty of all Life
And the mind will kiss the heart with unimaginable tenderness.

In those days
the Spirit of Christ shall breathe Love and Beneficence to all space
and Our Mother, our gentle Earth, shall be reunited totally and
indefeasibly with Our Father in Oneness –

As time melts into Eternity.

Becoming the Tranquil Sea

When you're centered in the all
The energy that comes to call
Is the quiet peace
Of expansive release.

For the emotions of up and down
Will no longer affect mind's crown
But balance each other in God centered ways
Wasting no energy through more primitive displays.

So rejoice in Heart's acceptance as each adventure begins anew
And smile at the invisible purposes ordained for You.

It Takes One to Know One

It takes one to know one.
It takes the spirit of gratitude to feel gratitude.
It takes the giving mind to receive the gifts of Love.

Sing and hear life's symphony
        Of morning's flowers kissing the sun –
        Of deer prancing in the meadows –
        And of trees dancing in the wind.
Smile and watch the faces around you light up in answer.

You're traveling Life's journey. . .

It takes Oneness to know Oneness.

Behind the Particulars

Of what importance be differing particulars that lead minds to The Goal
Of the Oneness and allness that Life can bestow~
For through the Doorway of Unified Peace
Blooms the Truth of Love's Wholeness, never to cease.

So live as loving children, guided by Heart's unhampered Way
Blessing all the particulars as you do each newborn day,
And Knowing beyond seeing, the Sonship within all
When Unity dissolves the separateness incurred by the fall --

Mind's Obedience

Mind is an amazing tool
And, in following Cosmic Laws, is no fool
But is often interfered with by the hand of man,
Who, in his ignorance, doesn't understand
The Universal Purpose for which he was created
And compromises True Values that his desires be sated.

But Mind, a knowing and beneficent caretaker,
Allows man this freedom while Honoring His Maker --
So that when the time is right,
Mind brings man's mistakes to Light.

Though Mind and Will are divine emanations
They are limited (by Law) to manifest creations
And are unable to interfere with Heart's High Resolve
For Man to Live the Purposeful Beauty ordained to evolve.

So in your life's creative play,
Look well at your choices each day.
Are they mainly to satisfy your fleeting desires
Or rooted in the unified Good to which Being aspires?
For if you can live in the Marriage of Heart and Mind
You'll find yourself and your world peaceful, loving and kind.

Gentle Thyself

When Thought is pure, it is devoid of polarities.
When Love is pure, it is devoid of attitudes.
So gentle thy thoughts and emotional responses,
For only in Peace,
can the Consciousness of Love
and the Purity of Thought
become ONE.

9: Reaching for the Teachings

Breathe Inspiration

Breathe inspiration into the minds of humanity
That persons help each other regale their sanity;
Then sing songs of confidence, love, and trust
That they'll awaken and sweep away their dust.

Let it be understood
That people are inherently good,
Ever desiring to do what's right
Unless they get caught up in fear, and fight.

Even then, by the singing in silence of purpose and grace,
Benevolence will come naturally our world to embrace —
That young innocents grow up with minds full of light
Where love and kindness overcomes fear and fright . . .

And the Peace in Patience swallows the stress of living
Allowing harmony and fruitfulness to dance in Life's giving.

Integrity's Integration

Are there hidden aspects to Integrity
That we claim to know through our mental sagacity?

Do we worship our integrity that we may stand on a high mountain
peak
Or give it the freedom if a more expansive good it would seek?

Only by letting go in faith and heart's Knowing
Will we gain the Wisdom that our Integration is sowing.

So be gentle with yourself and others who may not know where their
integration is at
For in mans world of becoming, nothing is this way or that.

Making Integrity Real

Can Integrity be de-fined
by mans outer mind
or is It an Indefinable Entity
of Immaculate Purity
residing between creation's polarity?

Only in the sweetness of our youth
do we claim to know God's Absolute Truth
in the Core of Love and Integrity.
Nevertheless, we must do our best
to make Its Actuality
the center of our reality.

Eat Well, See Well, Be Well

Cultivate your tastes, Inspire your desires,
And enliven your senses toward the Purposeful Higher.

To gratify your appetites isn't why you came
But to discover your true worth was your uppermost aim
To reflect loving kindness and creation's inner beauty
That's your reason for living and your God-given duty.

Sensationalism of any kind
Will offer you only the rind
Of the potential within you and life itself
And the inner fullness that's your true wealth.

So, in the quietness of your own being
Open to the Wonder beneath the seeming
And live in the magnificence of who you really are
Sharing the tenderness of the tiny flower within the Light of your star.

Honor Your Life

Honor your life and those persons and teachers who gave a part of their lives so that you should grow into the fullness of your Being. Honor them with Thanks Giving by not com-promising yourself, but by letting the Promise Come of the wondrous seeds they planted within you that they be lovingly fulfilled.

The Freedom of Forgiveness

The tiny bird begins his first flight half falling from his nest,
Yet even as he plummets down, he realizes that he's blest.

Things to explore & mistakes to be made intervene as time passes by
As he learns from experience what is good for him and how best to fly

At last, now mature, he looks once again on his life's earlier flights
And sees his mistakes, not as sinfully dark, but in a Purposeful Light.

Then looking at others, trying to create their life's way,
With true understanding for one & all, he soars in Freedom's New Day.

The Murmuring Brook

Mountain brook murmurings touch my soul
Smoothing earth's stones on the way to their goal:
That wondrous expanse of the Mother's Great Sea
That nurtures all life that is destined to be.

So, what if the stones that the stream displayed
Didn't challenge or interrupt the water's way --
Would the water be as clear when it sang to the trees?
Would its e-motions invite man to fall on his knees --

And learn of the Wonders its substance can bring
To nurture all creates through selfless offerings?
Sadly, to some, the stones simply get in the way,
But to the Knowing ones, they help initiate a new day.

Thought Forms

Our every thought finds a resonant space within our auric field
Then it's set in motion by emotion toward our world to be congealed.

Most don't really understand that at their command
                    are actors waiting in the wings,
To out-picture the play their thought-feelings display
                    and their power to manipulate things.

Would they enhance our perspectives
                  while mirroring our self and our objectives?
Would each gentle thought
                  grow the sweetness that is sought?
Or would it have to compete
                  for a clear-minded seat
With ill-tempered reactions which we have already bought?

The choice is ours, as young gods in the making,
                  With God not forsaking, to follow the patterns of Love,
Or stay captured by wants and follow their prompts
                  While forgetting Heaven's Beauty above.

I pray that we embrace our individual and world play
                  With thought forms of Kindness and Good,
And in that Loving Spirit, as we grow progressively near it,
                  Divine Guidance and Laws are lived and understood.

Your Security

Often you must go to the edge of your security
To discover your Heart's Power through Its innate Purity.

So when a challenge meets your gaze,
Be still to look beyond its obscuring haze ---

For Divine Law, God's Gift of Living Grace,
With unerring Justice regales Goodness in the human race ---

And giving Love to Life in Its perfect Purity,
Guides man to find True Peace and Security.

Judgements

It's by your judgements that you shall see you
And by their release that you shall see true
Then with an open heart and hand
You can walk the land as Man
In Peace, Love, and Understanding.

It's our judgements about a condition or experience that make it
personal and thereby energize our human emotions within it. As we free
ourselves of judgements, of good and bad, we can become impersonally
objective and be able to realize that what we are seeing is simply a
manifestation of a sine wave that is basic to all creation, helping us to
learn. When we can come to that point of experiential understanding
and knowing wisdom, the ups and downs of that sine wave will diminish
and neutralize into peace -- then, within that peace, we can see
Creation's Purposeful Laws in action and be grateful for their
deliverance which eventually assures our evolvement into Love,
Trust, and Truth.

From Honor to Love

Honor   Honor the GOD within each being and all that lives

Freedom   Give quiet freedom to the expansive Universal Field that IS and all within It.

Acceptance   Respect each individual, their place on their path, and their growth processes and experiences therein.

Understanding Stand under each experience so you can see the light of its origin and purpose shining through it.

Love   Gentle thy mind until it rests in the welcome expanse of Heart, there to feel the Presence, letting It flow that which is Beautiful, Blessed, and Bountiful from God's Wholeness

The Ultimate Progression

The foundation of this writing is Peace of Soul; Its carrier wave is Trust in The Wisdom of All Knowingness; and Its destination is all inclusive Love. Its Fulfillment results from realizing and letting go to The Greater Purpose and The Divine Destiny that each and all have inherited from Source.

The Ultimate Progression

1. The Oneness (Beneficent Beingness)
2. The Logos (a requirement for the Oneness to descend into Creation
3. The Great Purpose for the Going and the Return (the in breathing and out-breathing of Brahman) at the heart of The Logos (The Law)
4. The Field: Peace seeded with the underlying Great Purpose
5. The Carrier Wave: All inclusive Love and Trust
6. Pristine Creation descending into Divine Manifestation through:

> Love/Communion (come-Union) *Heart*
> Purpose/Direction *Mind*
> Trust/Peace: "Thy *Will* be done"

So, Beingness = Peace, seeded with Love and The Great Purpose
that holds all other purposes in Its bosom.

And by using this formula,
GOD (The Great One Denominator) blesses us all.

Consciousness

We think our consciousness is linear, but though it seems to be a consecutive live continuum, that is an illusion. We are continually shifting from & into different levels of consciousness, reflecting energies that we knew in the past or previewing energies that we will meet in future manifestation through differing states of consciousness..

Consciousness is spaceless and timeless, but we have been given a perspective of it that we can relate to in our human time space–time understanding. Like the young child who is given a small protected space by its parents, we are given the same grace. Eventually, we must expand this space. But, we've been taught distrust the world in the meantime, so we try to control this expansion, little realizing that the intervals between the thoughts and feelings we perceive are invisible and beyond the reach of our temporal minds. Now these intervals carry pure, clean, beneficent energy, but we can transform our perception of this energy through our fears and dominant thinking patterns.
The energy of doubt and fear or love and inspiration come to and through us every time we breathe – yet we hold on to this energy, thinking it is OURS that we have it and possess it, when it simply IS.

The problem might stem from our taking things too personally. We believe that the energy we awaken to in the morning is ours, never thinking that perhaps it is only loaned to us, not owned by us – For we know not whence comes this energy or even about the life force, values, and purposes within It. All we know is our descriptions of it – the labels we've put on it – religious, scientific, or speculative. This Energy is inherent in Consciousness – ever living, ever moving, ever changing – beyond linear and beyond any symbols that we can know. And with that consciousness we are in some mysterious manner wed. Therefore, we too are ever living, ever moving, ever changing when we let go of our smallness. Then we can sense and unite with the Integrity of the Law that underlies it. Then the energy that becomes us is made in Heaven.

Consciousness is not owned

But loaned

To all that we perceive

Or of which we can conceive

To Will of Not To Will

"Life is a conscious moral energy" (Manly P, Hall) -- Integrated, Beneficent, Purposeful, and Destined to bloom as simply and harmoniously as a wild flower opening her petals to the sun – **IF** it's natural energy isn't pressured or impeded by the force or underlying motives of mans will.

But why then was man given a free will? To be able to realize his self's full potential and have the capacity to attune and amalgamate his will with the Great All-Knowing Will. In this way, he can truly become aware of the intricate organization and orchestration of Creation and The Music of the Spheres that extends from the most minute particle to the wholeness of infinity, thereby awakening man to honor, trust, and serve that Will – that Invisible White Fire that glows around and through him, as Pure as Daath, the kabbalists' White Rose – Conscious, Integrated, Purposeful, and Destined to Bloom.

Integrity and Compassion

Integrity is a conduit to Truth. If I don't live in my integrity, how can I ever know or trust the truth of my being or of Higher Consciousness and GOD? -- for my integrity integrates me and my truth within the Absolute Truth and Integrity of GOD.

Now if GOD has Integrity within the beneficent field of Love, when there is suffering in the world, where resides 'His" Compassion?

GOD has given us a Way Shower within the Christ Spirit, but "He" also gave us free will. Thus "He" not only fore-gives us our miss-takes, but has prepared the means for us to overcome them. Through the Christ Spirit, through our soul and our inner self, we are given the right amount of energy at the perfect time and within perfectly orchestrated circumstances for us to correct (co-erect) our wrongs and heal ourselves in our own way -- and all the while, "He" is loving us with the tenderest compassion and blessing us with "His" Knowingness that we will Overcome and Be-come Whole.

Midnight Musings

When you look inside of yourself and you find what scares you,
you can also look deeper <u>to find what saves you</u>…

Your perceptive mind has been programmed to be able to see in a world of density – density being your captor and your protector. This mind has also been trained through ages of time to see surfaces and shadows, and to alert you through your emotions (again programmed energy movements) to potential disharmonies.

When you enter the realm of All Knowing, which we term the Universal Mind, you give up all mental and emotional constraints and constrictions inherent in particularization. The presence of this Universal Mind, berthing Its immaculate Laws, musical Harmonies, and sublime Ideals, is peaceful, open, transparent, and allowing.

As your emotions become at one with the Universal Mind, they automatically open and touch the Heart of all that lives in creation, and you will feel your own heart fill and expand within that combined resonance.

The Christ Consciousness is that perfected energy uniting the Universal Mind of The Father with the Sacred Heart of the Mother. It is Man's ordained destiny and the Saving Grace within you and all creation.

Today one can only catch glimpses of that Wondrous Glory, but those glimpses give you the Faith, the Trust, and the Knowingness <u>to find what saves you.</u>

Pro-seeding with Patience

Perform an action because it is the right thing to do; thereby it will have the freedom to represent Itself as a Purposeful Template in expanded consciousness.

Perform an action contaminated by self-interest, and it will attach itself to that self's psychic and be whirled around until its ramifications are experienced and transmuted by that self in its world.

True Purpose is always in alignment with the Fundamental Laws of Creation. Allow It Its inherent Freedom, trusting in the Wisdom, Guidance, and Divine Order within It, for within this Freedom will come Fulness, Wholeness, and Oneness.

Do what is right and be at Peace.

The Coming Messiah

The dream of the coming world teacher, The Messiah,
may not be a person but the essence of Good, of Love,
and of Righteousness within the Heart of all men.
This coming Savior, often known as The Lord Maitreya,
is the ever-growing Integrity in man himself, inspiring him
to serve the Integral Principles of GOD in his own heart.
Thus, collective humanity will be the embodiment of
The Buddha, The Christos, The True Being, which IS
and will be within, without, and ever present in mans time
as well as in Eternity.

Why Peace?

Why is Peace the conduit of Pure Energy and needed as a carrier of Prayer??

Like Pure Love, True Peace is directionless, having neither the push force (pressure) of the human mind's will nor its emotional intensities. Thus, True Peace can penetrate and cross through the myriad cells of polarized creation which have been lowered in vibration by the varying densities of the charges they are carrying. Because It (True Peace) goes directly through the heart of each cell's pristine, non-dimensional nucleus, it can slip through cell conglomerates of human creative impulses and pressured directions to retain Its Immaculate Vibratory State.

So when we want to commune with the Higher Dimensions of Value, Law, Beauty, Love, and Purpose in meditation or prayer, we should do so by attuning to (and becoming) Pure Peace and allowing Its Creative Energy and the All-Knowingness of Being to merge, thereby being assured that the Beneficent Destiny of the object(s) or condition(s) which instigated the prayer, be forthcoming on the Creative Planes, subsequently to echo down into manifestation in Divine Order and Perfect Timing.

The Language of Happiness

Leibnitz: To love is to place our happiness in the happiness of another

Helen Keller: Many persons have a wrong idea of what constitutes true
    happiness. It's not attaining through self-gratification, but
    through fidelity to a worthy purpose. Keep your face to the
    sunshine and you cannot see the shadow.

Oliver Windell Holmes: The great thing in this world is not so much
    where we are, but in what direction we are moving.

Albert Camus: In the midst of winter, I finally learned that there was in
    me an invincible summer.

Nathaniel Hawthorne: Happiness is a butterfly, which, when pursued,
    is always just beyond your grasp, but which, if you will sit down
    quietly, may alight on you.

Jane Porter: Happiness is a small sunbeam which may pass through a
    thousand bosoms without losing a particle of its original ray;
    nay, when it strikes on a kindred heart, like the converged light
    of a mirror, it reflects itself with redoubled brightness. It is not
    perfected until it is shared.

Manly P. Hall: Join God and through Love become a parent of the
    Great Light of the world. Become a creator of the blessedness
    in your heart.

Carena del Uno: Kneel before the kindly oak; caress the peace of
    morning's stillness; and give thanks for the fragile beauty of the
    tiny flower. All these and more are within you. Honor them.

Cycles of Change

Out of the night of ignorance
Mans will and control took its stance
Choosing wealth and gain through materiality
Over the love and wisdom of spirituality
Thus, our worldly conditions evolved from karmic pressures
Acting through Universal Justice, exacting in its measures.

Once again mans earned the right to choose
And in this cycle of Be-coming, he will not lose
For he took himself into the pit of unknowing
To redeem his mis-takes and begin the sowing
Of the Seeds of Light that are Destined to be
In the glorified Heart that's within you and me.

Finally, as we are able to bring ourselves into the fulness of this Divine
Order, so will our dedication to the Good, Freedom, and Gratefulness
help to free others still locked in the
fear that strict materiality is undergoing.

Beauty

Beauty lives within the sunshine of Being
And its lovelight enhances the world you are seeing

Be it a haven of miracles or a garden of Eden
It traverses realms holy through imagination's freedom.

Just be in resonance with that which you would abide
For that will determine the residence where it will reside

So have a wondrous day – Things are just fine
When you remain in the lovelight that allows Beauty to shine.

Growing Pains

Without experiencing a bounce, why would you challenge yourself to understand, to grow, and, eventually, to love?

The 5 categories of consciousness you must "No"/know:

No Comparison: Each entity has its own unique place on its path of evolvement toward its ordained template. Seldom are two or more entities on the same level, path, or area of development.

No Compromise: Gentle all situations with kindness whenever possible, but never compromise the Integrity residing in the Truth of your Heart.

No Competition: Unity, helpfulness, and harmony with The Good will open Invisible Doors to lasting Richness on every level. Competition leads to separateness which leads to powerlessness.

No Control: Control your self, your reactions, thoughts and emotions. With respect to that which has been divinely put into your sphere of influence follow your Divine direction, and for all else, trust and give your support to the Love and Wisdom of the Supreme Creator.

No Complaints: There is an immaculate intricacy in the subtle patterns within, behind, and composing each present now and flow of life according to the Beauty, Harmony, and Impeccability of Universal Law. Be grateful. If you must complain, complain to your self if you don't understand them.

My Bubble

My bubble just burst from self-made pressures, and my ego
went wallowing as hot air gushed from my balloon. I tried to
control a decision because of latent fears instead of trusting
and allowing freedom. Something little, you say? But no.
Forgiving myself and overcoming the challenge will come,
but it's greatest blessing is looking at all the people who have gone
through far greater challenges and have given the benefits of
their heroic selves in service to life.

Dear GOD, I'm so grateful to be part of our/Your humanity.

Sin

In Nature, sin is not forgiven -- It is outgrown
For no amount of platitudes can evaporate what you have sown.

Instead, you must return to sin's gate
And raise your mistake
Unto the standards you know to be right
In order to change its shadows into light.
Then its former tension will free your mind
And the dis-ease it engendered will be refined.

Now don't be constricted by a mistake you have caused
But look within, pray, and pause
And when similar leading patterns cycle 'round
Stand without compromise on Higher Ground

Living freely within your Integrity
Listening to your Soul's voice to guide your every choice
And exemplifying all that's Good and True
That resides eternally inside of You.

*This writing was inspired by Manly P. Hall

The Word Went Forth

And GOD spoke The Word, a creative vibration from the Wholeness of His Being, cradled in Beneficence and Love.

Every word creates a picture which can be set within a spring morning's meadow, a quiet forest glen, the nurturing of a mother's love, etc. The audible sound of that word will last but an instant in eternity, but its essence, its in-spoken spirit and the thoughts and feelings of its creator may last for generations to unite through love or divide through ignorance.

As sons of GOD, we strive to reach the life essence of words and use them as silent prayers to glorify life and uplift our world -- Words spoken from the God of our Hearts to the God of all creation: Gentle, Kindly, Beneficent – blessing us all.

Behold The Word

The vocal chords/cords are at the positive pole of the generative system, and a word is a vibratory form of generation whose vibration can go on forever, perpetuating manifestations upon manifestations.

Words form sacred patterns when they come from the soul; in fact, heart-felt prayer is the white magic of words.

So, feel the basic vitality of each word. Feel it within your chest singing as it dances within the etheric sweetness of Love. Recognize its <u>substance</u> – its true nature – its quality --- then let The Word go forth as the blessing It was meant to be.

P.S. *Though Mother Nature may not speak through words as man knows them, the sound of rain heals diseases of the heart and blood, the earth relaxes the mind and nervous system, and the sun promotes and regenerates cellular life.*

10: It's All Good

Halloween

Just remember, there's always a light within the pumpkin's face,
And the day after Halloween, all that's scary is enlightened by Grace.

    The witch's broomstick has swept the ground
    And to new heights, it's ready to rebound --
    Whereby the ghosts and goblins of your yesteryears
    Will begin to dissolve along with your fears.

    There's more Wisdom than you know
    Why All Saints Day follows Halloween's show

    So, fly high on your broomstick; blow your twin horns,

    A newer you is about to be born
    Endowed with more gratitude, trust, and understanding
    Within the Beneficent Love of God's commanding.

Giving Thanks

Wherever I am in a world of Grace
I reach out in fullness, in Light, Love, and Faith
That the flowers of spring eternally bloom
And to my worshipful Sovereign I keep attuned.

In a Garden of Beauty were we born
Its gentle offerings to adorn
While reflecting the sun's wondrous power
Throughout Mother Earth's living dower

So we give thanks even in the darkness of night
Forgetting not the Blessings of God's Purposeful Light
That conceived the Wonder and Glory that's meant to be
While honoring the Oneness within all that we see

Thus we give grateful Praise to each evolving star
For in Love's center, that's where we all are.

Values

What's the difference between the Art of Living and the Art of Dying?

Values.

Honor ~ Becoming
Growth ~ Beauty
Openness ~ Freedom –

Thoughts that rest on billowy white cushions of Love;
Hearts that reflect the warmth of each morning's sunrise;
Wonders that breathe in every leaf, every flower,
every tree that proclaims its Song. . .

These are the Values – Living Values –
Values that can never die.

And I thank Thee, Topside, for if I were dying, I know that You couldn't reach me with such inspired words, so though, when I was in the midst of the seemingly, unending granulated blackness of COVID's negation, though I felt like crying like a child, I allowed You, Hope, and Trust to remain at my door, Now I know more of What You Are than ever before.   And I thank Thee.

Outer Walls and Inner Temples

The crumbling of walls, and the building of temples
Rising naked and unafraid
Within the Knowing that Nature's Template has been laid. . .
Without haste; without measure –
Ever and always Destiny's treasure.

So welcome the flow; push not ahead,
But stand centered and tall like a tree instead.
Selfishness isn't just in the gathering of things
But believing that your tune is more important
Than what the other fellow sings.

Divide not The Truth. We are all One
In a purposeful array to reflect the Sun
And nurture the Beneficence that Mother Nature displays
In the simplicity and beauty of each newborn day.

Gentle down thy walls and build thee a Temple of Flowers
To honor the Love & Freedom of GOD's living dower.

Simple Beneficence

Simple Beneficence is the key
That unlocks the Life Force within us and all that we see
That opens realms of peace and understanding
Within the flow of Omniscient commanding.

So remove thy close (clothes) and allow Destiny unfathomable
To perfect thy Being through Its Will forever Spiritual
Knowing that the Wings of Beneficence
Will always lead us Home

Challenges

Welcome your challenges, trusting in the wonder of Life. Embrace them softly until you can go into the heart of them; then smile as all the fear, shame, anger, or guilt that guided them to you disperses like butterfly wings on a warm summer's eve. Only then will you know the Wonder of the Process, Divine Order, and God's perfect timing in all spiraled events.

An old adage says:
>"When the student is ready, the Master will appear."
"When the student is ready, the challenge will appear," is also true.

Re-cyst not, that imagined negativity perpetuate and hold you back from living your Heart's greatest Love-filled Ideal -- of serving GOD.

Ever There

I turned off my light and got to sleep about one
With a furry critter waking me up with the sun

Her bright feline eyes staring down at me in loving fun,
Her whiskers tickling my face, and her hair on my tongue.

But all that doesn't matter for during my night of deep dreaming,
a kindly masculine voice spoke of God's Presence streaming:

"EVER THERE."

Light

Light

Discern It

Learn It

And Earn It

To Become It

May we honor GOD

With every breath we breathe,
Every thought we think,
And every feeling we feel –

And may our Life glorify
The Living Altar of Love.

Peace

When you find your peace within,

You will also find its echo without –

No exclusions or blocks –

Open doors with no locks.

Resonance will guide your every step

That purposeful destinies may be kept

And rightful progressions will be done

On each man's journey toward The One.

About Carena del Uno

Dear Friends:

Following custom, I shall briefly sketch some points of my life, but please understand that the poems and teachings contained in this book did not originate with me, but came through me from a consciousness or consciousnesses is in a realm more knowing and expansive than my consciousness. Like you with in your life, I was prepared for this work and I'm very grateful for the uplifting words and feelings that accompanied it. That said, I was born in 1941 in San Francisco, California, to a father dedicated is giving his children every opportunity in life and a mother who was unconditionally loving. I joined the roster crucian order in 1965, the year my mother died, and became the pupil of Alma Genovese, a very psychic and spiritual RC lady wherein we studied mind and consciousness in depth in 1979, I became the co-founder of the Temple of Truth under the direction of Athena La Mer Marshand. Here I learned about God-love and heart. Many other knowing teachers pass through my life adding their beautiful light to my living tree. The latest of these teachers and one who has inspired many of the writings in this book was Manly P. Hall period finally I was fortunate enough to receive 12 years of university schooling, and, like you, have worked in the corporate world and have had my share of growing experiences. My favorite words are: "God Bless."

More books by Carena del Uno

Portals of Love

July 17, 2020

Inspirational, uplifting, spiritual poetry.

Echoes Within the Wondrous

March 17, 2017

The heavens sing of wonders yet unborn. The baby laughs in love and joy of the visions its yet to express. Then the child takes its first tentative steps in a new world – a world meant to echo the magnificence of That Which IS Eternally into that which will be in time. Eventually, the adult, remembering the Love and Unity of The Eternal, strives to keep Its Laws and integrate his being within It, thereby integrating his worlds through Love's Wisdom within The Wondrous.

This book echoes some of the wonders within us and around us through inspired poems that journey into love, integrity, openness and allowing, alternate realities, appreciation, thankfulness, and more. Inner Streaming: Esoteric Teachings in Poetic Form November 24, 2015

Channeled esoteric teachings written in a poetic format. Each of these poems contained a key to the solution of one or more challenges that had to be mastered in higher consciousness to assure a positive living manifestation.

Welcoming Oneness

January 22, 2013

Welcoming Oneness is not only the title but the theme of this book, and that Oneness must include the unseen realms we call spiritual as well as the seen realm. The poems make up a bouquet of unfolding fl owers, whereby each fl ower, having found a tiny crack in the wall of self, saw a light and reached for it. Then, after going through the learning experience of pushing the wall's old concepts and feelings aside, rays from that light warmed each fl ower's petals until they opened unto its heart, and a poem was born. Thus each poem was not the work of mind alone, but an experiential creation, beginning from deep inside the heart, seeding yearning and aspirations, and fi nally traveling into the sphere of expanding consciousness whereby it could be lived. As such, each page might hold a treasure that can be a lesson in itself, opening ones heart or mind into beauty or lifting one out of a space that is unworthy of their wondrous being.

In the Heart of Forever

July 9, 2013

Just as the life force of a young green sprout pushes upward to open a crack in the sidewalk, so does the Divine Field of Energy within us break through our walls to expose us to the Sunlight of Love and the Joy of Life. Thus the many challenges we face are but part of the unveilings of the seeds of Truth within us, growing and expanding our awareness toward heaven's glorious Ideals. Each page of this book records the result of a blessed unfolding. Each is a gentle reminder of the Goodness that is our divine inheritance. May their expressions warm your heart and enlighten your mind to the Beauty that IS, ever and eternally. * * * In my search for the meaning of life, these poems are my journal. In my search for Truth, these poems are quiet echoes from Infinite Consciousness. In my search for Love, these poems reveal Heart's innate tenderness. In my search for GOD, this is what I found - In The Heart of Forever.